COUNTRY LIFE

PICTURE BOOK
OF LONDON

WESTMINSTER BRIDGE AND THE HOUSES OF PARLIAMENT, FROM LONDON'S COUNTY HALL

COUNTRY LIFE
PICTURE BOOK
OF LONDON

WITH AN INTRODUCTION BY

JOHN CODRINGTON

COUNTRY LIFE LIMITED

2-10 TAVISTOCK STREET, COVENT GARDEN

LONDON W.C.2

First published in 1951
by Country Life Limited
Tavistock Street London W.C.2
Process engraving by
The Sun Engraving Co. Ltd London
Printed in Great Britain by
Balding & Mansell Ltd
London & Wisbech

Second Impression 1951

LONDON

LONDON is a name all the world knows, and every year from every country come thousands of visitors to see London.

But how many of these visitors go away with a slight sense of disappointment? London has few of the splendid wide avenues and long vistas of Paris, few of the beauties of past centuries such as crowd upon the visitor to Rome. She cannot boast the baroque of Vienna or the arresting skyline of New York, and her charm does not jump to the eye of the new arrival.

Yet London has 'something', though it is a 'something' that is not immediately obvious. The visitor has to dig for it and sense it gradually. That is why quite a number of people with somewhat superficial minds, or in too much of a hurry for quick effects, miss the point of London and are apt to be disappointed.

The pictures in this book set out to help such people to realize the soul and unexpected beauty of this great town which is a county containing two cities, twenty-seven boroughs and many suburbs besides, and which is also the largest port in the world besides being the capital of the British Empire and Commonwealth of Nations.

How did it all happen? To appreciate London properly a quick glance through its history is essential; then things that at first seemed puzzling fall into their proper places.

London began because of the River Thames. It is not a very long river, as rivers go, but it has a wide and deep estuary with a tide that rises and falls some fifteen feet and keeps the channel dredged and navigable right into the heart of the City

The Romans, the Saxons, the Danes and the Normans all appreciated this, and the Romans built their City with its forum and temples on the heights on the north bank of the Thames. They built a wall around it, parts of which are still to be seen today, and which extended roughly in a semi-circle with a radius of about half a mile from London Bridge.

After the Romans left Britain, London lay derelict for a long time. Some of the ancient British and Celtic inhabitants began to drift back, but they could not withstand the Saxon pirates who came in from the sea and gradually settled round the Roman ruins in 'tons' or fortified villages (such as Charlton, Islington, Paddington, Kensington, Kennington) or homesteads or 'hams' (such as Clapham, Eltham, West and East Ham, Fulham, Hampstead).

The part of this great town known as the City of London to this day roughly corresponds to the area of the old Roman City of Londinium; and her twisting streets probably follow the tracks which the Saxon shepherds made with their sheep. And the great estuary up which sailed St Olaf of Norway and Cnut the Dane and all the commerce from across the North Sea is still the foundation of the importance of the City.

But meanwhile another influence of London's destiny was in the making. About a mile and a half upstream to the west from London Bridge, on a desolate island covered with thorns and brambles in the marshes, some monks founded a monastery. Already in the City of London a cathedral dedicated to St Paul was arising; the monastery on Thorney Island became the monastery or minster in the west, and today we know its successor as Westminster Abbey. The saintly king, Edward the Confessor, enriched and endowed the abbey, making his palace nearby. The church has been rebuilt several times since his day, but his body still lies in his shrine behind the High Altar of the great church of St Peter in Westminster.

The royal connexion endured. The kings of England have lived in Westminster on and off for some nine hundred years and have all—except Edward V and Edward VIII—been crowned in the Abbey. In 1900 Westminster was given the title of 'City', and is thus the second city within the town of London. The City (of London) itself is the historic core of this great place, and the heart of its trade and commerce today as it has been all down the ages, while the City of Westminster is, and has always been, the seat of Goverment and the residence of the monarch and court.

Gradually the City of London became so congested that many of the wealthier inhabitants and peers of the realm built riverside houses and palaces along the strand or foreshore of the Thames upstream towards Westminster, where the court was, and so gradually the link-up between the two cities took place along what is still called The Strand.

Over against the City of London on the south bank of the river was the southern outwork or bulwark defending the approaches to London Bridge. It became the first suburb or borough outside the walls, and the borough of Southwark is still known as *the* Borough to all Londoners, and has a history almost as ancient as the parent city. It now has its own cathedral for the vast area of present-day London south of the Thames.

Gradually the little Saxon hamlets and villages became joined to the central masses of London and Westminster. In Charles I's reign the laying out of Covent Garden and Lincoln's Inn Fields under the supervision of Inigo Jones gave London its first regularly planned open spaces with houses ranged round them which are so characteristic of our metropolis. The arcaded houses of Covent Garden have been pulled down and the vegetable market now covers most of the open space, but Jones's church, St Paul's, still stands at the west end, albeit reconstructed after a fire. The Great Fire of London in 1666 necessitated the rebuilding of the greater part of the City. For half a century building activity was concentrated on this formidable task and so, while St Paul's was slowly rising and Wren's steeples were taking their places one by one on the London sky-line, the outward expansion of the metropolis was inevitably slowed down; but already before the Fire the first London squares to be so called—Bloomsbury Square and St James's Square—had begun to take shape. The characteristic London house, simple, restrained and dignified, with beautifully designed doorway and graceful ironwork, made its appearance.

For a century and a half, with but slight modifications arising from changes in taste and fashion, the typical London house continued to take its place in street and square as these multiplied in Bloomsbury and Mayfair and farther out beyond Oxford Street. The outward pressure was growing under the first two Georges, but it was immensely increased during the long reign of George III, to which most of the Georgian squares of London belong. No other capital city, Dublin and Edinburgh excepted, can parallel this remarkable achievement in town-planning, effected with typical English reticence and absence of display, and using for the most part workaday brick instead of stone or marble. The growth of London produced a need for new churches. Some, like St Martin-in-the-Fields, were rebuilt in classical dress, but many more—the graceful St Mary-le-Strand, for instance, and St George's, Hanover Square—were new creations, built in the white Portland stone which Wren had used so effectively in the City.

Early in the nineteenth century, with London ever spreading outwards, came the age of stucco, and the period of the Prince Regent and Nash to whom we owe the magnificent town-planning scheme which, beginning at Waterloo Place with the Duke of York's Column and Carlton House Terrace, culminates in Regent's Park with its terraces. Many other squares (grand, like Belgrave Square; modest like Victoria Square) and many more terraced streets came later. Meanwhile the surrounding villages were gradually absorbed into the mass and in many cases have become the boroughs of today with no green fields between them. The old village centre, with its green, its High Street, its parish church and its pubs can almost always still be identified, and the boroughs generally still keep that sturdy feeling of independence that is so characteristic of villages in the country.

So London goes on growing, each generation adding to it in its own style and its own way; some of it good— a lot of it bad. Almost always the development has been piecemeal, and the result of a sturdy individualism on the part of land-owners or speculative builders. London has never had an overall plan (Wren's plan for the City after the Great Fire was turned down).

And now London, battered almost ceaselessly during the last war, is rising again and is erecting new and, we hope, better buildings. The bombing destroyed much that was beautiful and old, but also much that was a perpetual disgrace to the largest city in the world. One may hope that the Londoners of the next generation will not need to be so critical of their forbears as we must often be.

It is chiefly the purpose of this Picture Book of London to help visitors to appreciate the many aspects of this great metropolis. We start with the splendid palace built by Sir Christopher Wren at Greenwich, the first of the many unexpected wonders for the traveller who comes up the Thames from the sea. We move past the Tower Bridge, that great portal to the City, a rare example of Victorian imagination, and a monument to the prosperity of the age; on to The Pool with its shipping from all over the world; and on to the Tower, the great fortress that has guarded the entrance to the City since William I's reign and has been fortress, palace and political prison ever since. (Certain traitors were imprisoned here in both the recent World Wars.)

From the grandeur of the Tower we pass to the humble waterside pub, to the City merchants, the brokers of Throgmorton Street, and the fish porters of Billingsgate—each of them different aspects of the great hive that is London. A few pictures show us the past of the City, while the 'Clink' takes us back to the grim prison (destroyed in the Gordon Riots of 1780) which gives its name to prisons wherever the English language is spoken. The City, with St Paul's dominating it, leads us from commerce to the Law, and to the Temple (in whose gardens two angry dukes are said to have plucked red and white roses centuries ago, and so started a useless but bloody civil war), and the Inns of Court. London is then seen as the centre of a famous university with the British Museum nearby, while onwards our Picture Book takes us upstream to Westminster and Whitehall with their Royal Palaces and Government Offices.

Next, in the West End, are London's theatres and places of amusement, and the lights of Piccadilly and Leicester Square, which, though on a modest scale compared with those of New York and many other cities, are much loved by Londoners. And these same Londoners love the country; they take great slabs of the countryside and enclose it with all its natural life into their town. Here sheep graze and blackbirds sing in the parks, swans and wild duck swim on the lakes, and the trees are not clipped.

Yet London does have its hours of pomp and ceremony, and the wide streets round the Royal Palaces are suitable for the splendid ceremonial and gay uniforms of the Household Troops. And so we pass through the quiet, once aristocratic West End on to literary Chelsea and Hampstead. Peacefulness and serenity are shown in the rest of the book, with the splendidly contrasting bulk of the Power Station at Chelsea to remind us that in West London there is the same throbbing energy and vitality as there is in the City and among the docks.

Thus we show this immense town as a panorama of many aspects. It is to be hoped that the visitor's appetite may be stimulated by these pictures and that he will explore and find many other equally entrancing and varied aspects of London for himself.

1951   JOHN CODRINGTON

LIST OF PLATES

ACKNOWLEDGEMENTS

Acknowledgements are due to the following who provided the photographs for this book:

G. F. Allen, *frontispiece*, plates 1, 6, 7, 9-17, 19, 23, 25, 30, 34, 43, 48, 52-54, 56-59, 67, 76-81, 83, 86-88

Sport and General, *plate* 4; Central Press, *plate* 37; Graphic Photo Union, *plate* 40; Photographic News Agencies, *plate* 46.

All other illustrations are from *Country Life* photographs.

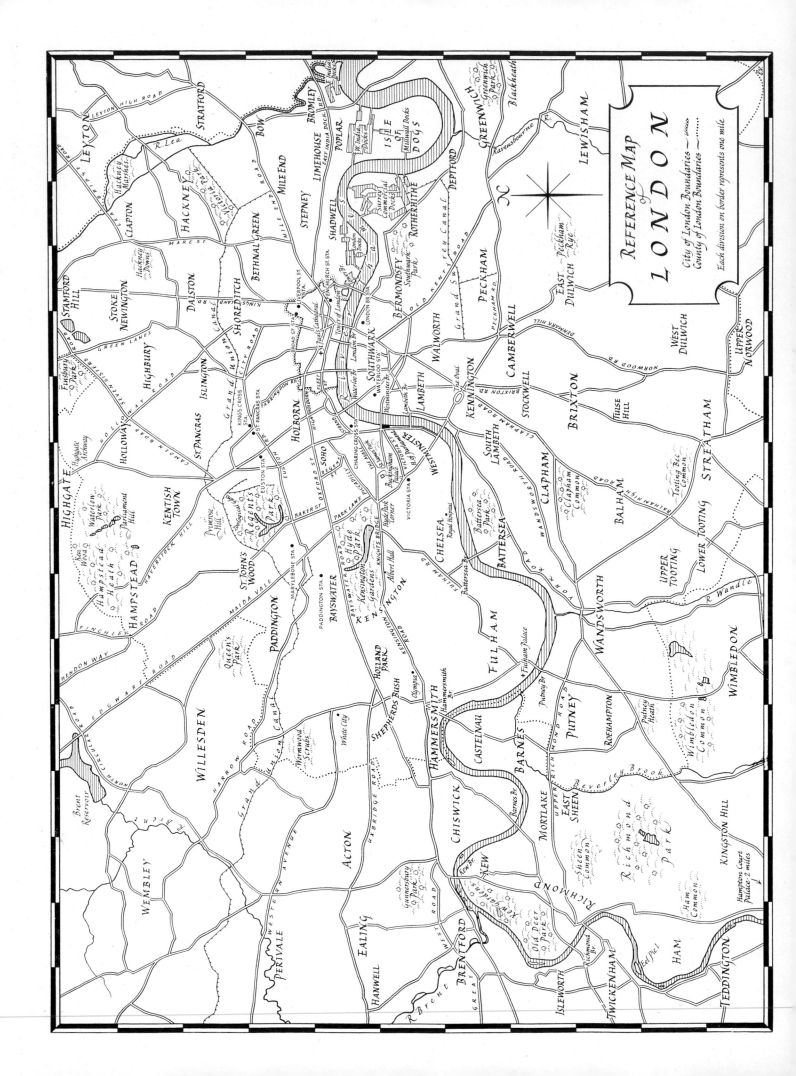

REFERENCE MAP
of
LONDON

City of London Boundaries —
County of London Boundaries —

Each division on border represents one mile

1. THE ROYAL HOSPITAL, GREENWICH. This noble group of Thames-side buildings, now the home of the National Maritime Museum and the Royal Naval War College, was begun by Charles II and completed to the designs of Sir Christopher Wren in the reign of William III.

2. TOWER BRIDGE, LOOKING DOWN-RIVER. Tower Bridge is the last bridge down the Thames. Beyond it lie London's great docks, and the highway to the sea. The bridge, with its raised footway 142 feet above high water, and the twin leaves of its central span, was opened in 1894.

3. **THE POOL OF LONDON.** A view of one of the busiest sections of the river, looking west towards London Bridge. The skyline of the north bank is dominated by the Monument, to the right of which, facing the river, is the Custom House.

4. THE YEOMAN WARDERS OF THE TOWER. Led by the Chief Warder, the Yeoman Warders, in their scarlet uniforms and Tudor bonnets, march in procession within the precincts of the Tower that has been guarded by this famous corps for more than four hundred years.

5. THE WHITE TOWER ON TOWER HILL.   The White Tower is the heart of the great fortress of the Tower of London. Built by William the Conquerer, its walls and battlements have been the settings for some of the most tragic episodes in British history.

6. 'THE PROSPECT OF WHITBY', WAPPING. This picturesque dockland inn takes its name from one of the ships out of the Yorkshire town of Whitby which, in former years, anchored here at the end of their coast-wise voyages.

THE MONUMENT. The two-hundred-foot column of Wren's memorial to the Great Fire of 1666 rises above streets crowded by the porters of nearby Billingsgate—for hundreds of years London's chief fish market.

8. THROGMORTON STREET. This street, which lies just behind the Bank of England, is the 'home' of London's stockbrokers. Its name recalls a Tudor statesman who was instrumental in bringing Lady Jane Grey to the throne, and was father-in-law of Sir Walter Raleigh.

9. ST MARY-LE-BOW, CHEAPSIDE. Only those born within the sound of the bells of this famous old city church are truly Londoners born. The steeple is generally considered to be the finest of those designed by Sir Christopher Wren after the Great Fire.

10. IRONMONGERS' HALL.   The City of London is rich in the buildings that are the headquarters of its ancient companies. The Hall of the Ironmongers is a recent building, replacing one destroyed by a bomb in the First World War.

11. ST JOHN'S GATE, CLERKENWELL. This was once the gateway of the Priory of the Knights of St John of Jerusalem, and was built in 1504, not many years before the Order was dissolved. Now it is once more the headquarters of the Knights of the revived Order.

12. THE 'TIGER' INN, TOWER HILL. An inn of this name was standing on the site of the present building as far back as 1500, and the tradition that Queen Elizabeth visited it on her way down-river to Tilbury in 1556 is still remembered.

3. ON BANKSIDE. Early morning, among the cranes and warehouses on the south bank of the river. Through the mist can be seen the outlines of Southwark Bridge and, beyond it, the arched roof of Cannon Street Station.

14. CLINK STREET, SOUTHWARK. Bankside, where once stood Shakespeare's 'Globe', is now a place of tall warehouses and narr grimy passages. Clink Street takes its name from the 'clink' or prison administered here in medieval times by the Bishops of Winchest

LONDON BRIDGE AND SOUTHWARK CATHEDRAL. London Bridge as we know it was built in 1831. At its southern end stands Southwark Cathedral, famous for its associations with Shakespeare and his friends, and many other great names in English Literature.

16. THE BANK OF ENGLAND.   The Bank, in the heart of the City, was established at the end of the seventeenth century. The great n
building, added to the old in this century, was designed by Sir Herbert Baker.

17. THE ROYAL EXCHANGE.   The present building, opened by Queen Victoria in 1844, is the third to occupy the site since its foundation
in 1571. From its steps the accession of a new sovereign is proclaimed in the City of London.

18. FLEET STREET. The view is that towards Ludgate Hill and St Paul's. Here, or nearby, are the headquarters of most of England's national newspapers and news-gathering organizations. Its name comes from the old Fleet river, now dwindled into an underground drain.

19. ST PAUL'S, FROM SOUTH BANK. The dome of St Paul's Cathedral is the noblest sight in London's skies. The Cathedral is Wren's master-work; the splendid memorial of the new London which arose from the ashes of the old after the Great Fire.

20. THE LAW COURTS. This impressive memorial of the Gothic revival of the nineteenth century was completed in 1882. It faces the Strand, just beyond 'the Griffin' which stands on a pedestal in the middle of the road and marks the beginning of Fleet Street.

1. THE STRAND. The view towards the eighteenth-century church of St Mary-le-Strand, with St Clement Danes behind it, is known all over the world, and the street itself, as much as any other in London, stands as an image of London to travellers and to exiles in distant places.

22. EXCHANGE COURT, STRAND. Many discoveries are to be made by the Londoner who turns aside from the main streets. Exchange Court, just off the Strand, is notable for its imposing eighteenth-century house, since 1859 the headquarters of the Corps of Commissionaires

. IN NEW SQUARE, LINCOLN'S INN, HOLBORN.   Lincoln's Inn is one of the four Inns of Court which alone have the authority to call new recruits 'to the bar'. New Square is a gracious open space enclosed by pleasant office buildings of brick.

24. MIDDLE TEMPLE LANE.   This narrow passage-way, which runs between Fleet Street and the Thames Embankment, approximat
divides the territories of the two great Inns of the Temple, Inner and Middle Temple.

25. MIDDLE TEMPLE HALL. This majestic hall was opened by Queen Elizabeth in 1572. Here she danced, and here Shakespeare is believed to have acted in 'Twelfth Night' in 1602. The superbly carved oak screen and gallery are of the same age as the hall.

26. **UNIVERSITY OF LONDON, HOLBORN.** The great white tower of London's great centre of learning rises 210 feet in Bloomsbury's skies. The designer of this as yet unfinished group of buildings is Mr Charles Holden, whose work began in 1931.

27. **THE BRITISH MUSEUM, HOLBORN.** A corner of one of the world's greatest stores of art-treasures, which is seen by hundreds of thousands of scholars, students and visitors every year. The collection was begun in 1753 with the purchase of manuscripts assembled by Sir Hans Sloane.

28. ST PANCRAS CHURCH, EUSTON ROAD. This church, the work of William Inwood in 1820, is unique in London, and perhaps in England, for its faithful rendering of the strict Greek style. The design of the tower is based on that of the Athenian 'Tower of the Winds'.

29. IN GORDON SQUARE, BLOOMSBURY. The area of London that lies between the Euston Road and New Oxford Street is a famous centre of learning and study. It owes its charm to its many quiet squares enclosing the tree-shaded lawns and flower-beds of their gardens.

30. ON THE EMBANKMENT. 'Discovery', once commanded by Scott of the Antarctic, and veteran of many years of Polar voyages, was moored below Waterloo Bridge in 1937 as a memorial to Captain Scott and his comrades and as a training ship of the Scouts Association

31. CLEOPATRA'S NEEDLE, EMBANKMENT. This famous granite column, first hewn about 1450 B.C., erected before the great temple of Heliopolis in Egypt, and then moved to Cleopatra's palace in Alexandria, was brought to this country after an adventurous sea voyage in 1878.

32. WATERLOO BRIDGE. The view from South Bank of the most modern of the great Thames bridges, designed by Sir Giles Gilbert Scott. It was opened in 1945 to replace John Rennie's old bridge—one of the most beautiful in Europe—whose foundations were discovered to be unsafe in the nineteen-twenties.

33. WESTMINSTER BRIDGE. Looking west from the Embankment to the bridge which was opened not long after the completion of the Houses of Parliament, in 1862, there is this spacious view of London's County Hall (extreme left) and the turreted blocks of St Thomas's Hospital whose history of healing goes back for more than seven hundred years.

34. HENRY VII'S CHAPEL, WESTMINSTER ABBEY. This chapel is the most glorious part of the Abbey, and its vaulted roo
one of the supreme masterpieces of church architecture. It was begun in 1502, and within it are the tombs of many British Kings and Queen

35. THE STATUE OF OLIVER CROMWELL, WESTMINSTER HALL. The splendid statue of the great Protector stands before Westminster Hall where he was proclaimed Protector. The Hall dates from 1097, in the time of William Rufus.

36. WHITEHALL. The view of this famous street is that towards Big Ben and the Houses of Parliament. Its name stands everywhere f
the government of Great Britain and the Commonwealth—for in or around it are all the great administrative offices of the State.

37. THE CENOTAPH. His Majesty the King, members of the Royal Family, Cabinet ministers, and a great gathering of people in every walk of life attend the annual remembrance of the dead of two world wars at the Cenotaph, the Commonwealth's memorial in Whitehall.

38. NUMBER TEN, DOWNING STREET.   The unpretentious façade of one of the best-known houses in the world. Number Ten, the official residence of the Prime Minister, has formed part of the group of Treasury buildings since the eighteenth century.

39. KING CHARLES STREET, WHITEHALL. The view towards St James's Park through one of the arches of the bridge that onnects the huge blocks of Government offices between Downing Street and Parliament Square. All have been built in the last hundred years.

40. A STATE OPENING OF PARLIAMENT. The royal coach, carrying His Majesty the King to Westminster, turns into Whitehall from Horse Guards Parade. Behind the procession is the Horse Guards itself, an eighteenth-century building guarded by mounted sentries of the Household Cavalry.

41. **WHITEHALL FROM ST JAMES'S PARK.** The tower of the Foreign Office building seen across a corner of the lake of the most enchanting of London's parks. It was first emparked by Henry VIII who maintained in it a herd of deer.

42. ST JAMES'S PARK: THE LAKE.   The lake (from whose central suspension bridge there is one of the loveliest views in London)
stretches almost the whole length of the Park, and is the home of many rare and beautiful kinds of wildfowl.

3. WESTMINSTER CATHEDRAL. The campanile of the great Roman Catholic cathedral commands an unequalled view of Greater
ondon. The vast building of red brick and white stone was designed by J. F. Bentley, and its first stone was laid by Cardinal Vaughan in 1895.

44. CONSTITUTION HILL, GREEN PARK. The King's Guard of the Royal Horse Guards rides down Constitution Hill to Whitehall. At its back is Decimus Burton's archway ... the Hill ... one of the most beautiful of London's sculptere groups. Adrian Jones's 'Quadriga', erected to the memory of Edward VII.

45. DUKE OF YORK'S STEPS. At the foot of the Duke of York's column, a broad flight of steps leads into the Mall and, beyond it, to St James's Park. Facing the steps is the Royal Artillery Memorial to the dead of the South African war.

46. LONDON'S GREAT PROCESSIONAL WAY. The scene from Buckingham Palace as His Majesty the King, with an escort of the Household Cavalry, drives past the Victoria Memorial and into the Mall for the ceremony on Horse Guards Parade of Trooping the Colour, which annually marks his official birthday.

47. THE CHANGING OF THE GUARD AT BUCKINGHAM PALACE. Headed by the band of the Irish Guards, the new guard marches before the gates of the Palace to take up its duties. The Royal Standard flying above the Palace is a sign that the King is in residence.

48. CLARENCE HOUSE, ST JAMES'S.　　The view from Clarence Gate of the London home of Princess Elizabeth and the Duke of Edinburgh. This gracious house, facing the Mall, was rebuilt early in the nineteenth century, and was once the home of King William IV.

9. ST JAMES'S PALACE. The Tudor palace of St James's, begun for Henry VIII, is no longer the home of the sovereign; but it is still to 'Our Court of St James's' that ambassadors from foreign countries are accredited.

50. LEICESTER SQUARE. The square owes its fame to its nineteenth-century theatres (now all replaced by cinemas), and not to any elegance in its design. but the garden surrounding a statue of Shakespeare makes an attractive oasis in the heart of the West End.

51. THE HAYMARKET. This street, which is the principal traffic link between Trafalgar Square and Piccadilly Circus, is distinguished for the charming portico of the Theatre Royal, designed early in the nineteenth century by John Nash, architect of Old Regent Street.

52. TRAFALGAR SQUARE. The view of this famous square is of its eastern side: on the right the façade of South Africa House; on the left the portico and spire of St Martin-in-the-Fields, designed by James Gibbs in 1726.

53. PICCADILLY CIRCUS. Few monuments are more widely known or better loved than Sir Alfred Gilbert's 'Eros', poised above the fountain which stands at the busy heart of London's West End. It was set up as a memorial to the great humanitarian, the Earl of Shaftesbury.

54. SHEPHERD MARKET, WESTMINSTER. This small corner of Mayfair is one of the most surprising survivals in London, for here, just off Piccadilly, the visitor finds himself among the shops and narrow streets of a small country town of the eighteenth century.

5. IN CURZON STREET, MAYFAIR. This attractive front hints at the elegance of a street which runs west to Park Lane through Mayfair, a name symbolic of London's wealth and fashion all over the world.

56. PICCADILLY, FROM HYDE PARK CORNER. Apsley House is the first of these great houses which overlook Green Park at the western end of Piccadilly. It was presented by the nation to the Duke of Wellington after the battle of Waterloo.

7. THE 'QUADRIGA': HYDE PARK CORNER. In this view of one of the busiest traffic centres in the world, the 'Quadriga' looks down on Charles Jagger's massive and sombre memorial, now dedicated to the men of the Royal Artillery who died in two world wars.

58. 93, PARK LANE. Built in 1827, this is one of the last survivors of the Regency houses of Park Lane, now known for its great modern hotels and office buildings. This was the London home of Disraeli from 1839 to 1873.

9. HYDE PARK CORNER. The view, over Decimus Burton's graceful triple-arched entrance screen, of the Hyde Park roadway leading to the Marble Arch. The screen, built in 1826, is adorned with reliefs copied from those of the frieze of the Parthenon.

60. THE SERPENTINE, HYDE PARK. This long, artificial sheet of water, created by Queen Caroline, wife of George II, is the Londoner's own 'lido' where, in the heat of

61. IN HYDE PARK. London has many lovely parks and gardens, but in none is it more fortunate than in the great open space of Hyde Park. There are upwards of 400 acres of it—which explains why this might be a scene deep in the countryside, a hundred miles from London.

62. GROSVENOR SQUARE.   The character of this famous Georgian square in Mayfair has greatly changed in recent years. It was almost completely transformed in 1948 when the statue of President Roosevelt was set up facing an open space of green lawns.

63. REGENT STREET.   The massive buildings of one of the world's finest shopping centres sweeping from Piccadilly Circus to Oxford Street, are a twentieth-century replacement of John Nash's original Regent Street, laid out between 1813 and 1820.

64. BROADCASTING HOUSE, PORTLAND PLACE. The striking headquarters of the B.B.C. occupies an island site at the northern end of Regent Street. Above the entrance is Eric Gill's sculpture of Prospero and his 'brave spirit' Ariel.

THE LAKE IN REGENT'S PARK. This exquisite park—the home of the Zoo and London's Open Air Theatre—is less than a mile north of Oxford Circus. It was laid out early in the nineteenth century for the Prince Regent by John Nash.

66. KENWOOD, HAMPSTEAD. Left to the nation in 1927 by Lord Iveagh, Kenwood House preserves, on the edge of Hampstead Heath, a fine example of an eighteenth-century country house, with a notable collection of pictures, in a splendid landscape of the period

CHURCH ROW, HAMPSTEAD. The suburb of Hampstead on its steep hill to the north of London retains much of the grace and auty of its past as a village and fashionable spa. Church Row, with its dignified Georgian houses, is at the heart of 'village' Hampstead.

68. THE ROYAL ALBERT HALL. The view from Kensington Road of London's largest hall in which there is room for up to 10,000 people to hear a concert, watch a prize-

69. IN WILTON CRESCENT, WESTMINSTER. A view typical of the quiet and still elegant quarter between Knightsbridge and Buckingham Palace Road, called Belgravia. The church in the background is St Paul's, Knightsbridge, built in the middle of the nineteenth century.

70. IN ROTTEN ROW. This well-known ride stretches for more than a mile from Hyde Park Corner through Hyde Park. The name is said to be a corruption of 'route du roi'—the King's Way.

1. KENSINGTON GARDENS.   The gardens adjoin Hyde Park, but preserve their identity to the point of using the name 'Long Water' to describe their stretch of the Serpentine. Overlooking this water is Sir George Frampton's well-loved statue of Peter Pan.

72. WILTON PLACE, BELGRAVIA. The squares and streets of this area are among the best examples of early nineteenth-century building left to London. They date from about 1820–30 on a site transformed by a great builder of the time, Thomas Cubitt.

3. CANNING PLACE, KENSINGTON. The view of Kensington Gate from Canning Place, whose name recalls the fact that the statesman George Canning lived nearby in the second decade of the nineteenth century.

74. IN KENSINGTON GATE. The imposing houses of this small square off the Gloucester Road were built in 1850, thus demonstratin
that not all Victorian building was lacking in elegance and architectural good manners.

KYNANCE MEWS, KENSINGTON. London's many picturesque mews are survivals from the days of the horse. The stables now
ther house motor-cars or have been converted into flats. The towers in the background of this photograph are of the Imperial Institute.

76. CHEYNE WALK, CHELSEA. One of the loveliest rows of houses in London, Cheyne Walk faces the Thames and has been the ho[me] of many famous writers and artists, among them George Eliot, Rossetti, and Thomas Carlyle.

77. THE ROYAL HOSPITAL, CHELSEA. The portico and cupola of the main building of the home in London of the scarlet-coated veterans of Britain's armies. It was founded in 1682 by Charles II, and designed (though since altered and enlarged) by Sir Christopher Wren.

78. IN GLEBE PLACE, CHELSEA.   Not many generations have passed since Chelsea was one of London's 'villages', and here and there the passer-by may still come across corners such as this, which might belong to the high street of a village deep in the country.

79. LOTS ROAD POWER STATION, CHELSEA. Chelsea's river front is not all a stretch gracious with trees and dignified houses. The chimneys (275 feet high) of its huge power station make an impressive monument of the Age of Electricity.

80. THE COURTYARD OF FULHAM PALACE. The palace on the north bank of the Thames has been for hundreds of years the home of the Bishops of London. The courtyard, with its diamond pattern of black bricks on red, was built in the early years of the reign of Henry VIII.

LAMBETH PALACE. The view across the Thames of the Tudor gatehouse (and beyond it, the old church of St Mary's) of the palace that has for seven hundred years been the residence in London of the Archbishops of Canterbury.

82. CHISWICK HOUSE.   The flights of steps leading to the portico of the famous Palladian retreat built on Thames-side by Lor
Burlington between 1727 and 1736. The park which surrounds it is the noblest of Chiswick's open spaces.

LOWER MALL, HAMMERSMITH. The Mall is certainly the most delightful part of Hammersmith—most westerly of London's boroughs. Its balconied Georgian houses are legacies of a time when this was a summer retreat for fashionable Londoners.

84. IN KEW GARDENS. These glorious gardens on the south bank of the Thames are, at any time of the year, one of the 'sights of London'—though strictly speaking beyond

85. STRAND-ON-THE-GREEN, CHISWICK. Strand-on-the-Green, immediately east of Kew Bridge, was once a Thames-side village. This stretch of its water-front owes much of its charm, however, to the grace of its Georgian houses.

86. 'THE LONDON APPRENTICE', ISLEWORTH. Barges still dock at Isleworth water-front near this famous old inn, as they have been doing for hundreds of years. The name recalls the days when City apprentices rowed up to this place on high days and holidays.

37. RICHMOND BRIDGE, SURREY.   The bridge has been widened since James Paine designed it in 1777; but it remains unspoiled, like Richmond itself whose views of the Thames are unsurpassed in variety and grandeur by those of any other reach of the river.

88. HAMPTON COURT PALACE. The view from Sir Edwin Lutyens's bridge over the Thames of the great royal palace begun by Cardinal Wolsey and 'presented' by him to Henry VIII. Besides much splendid Tudor work, it displays some of the best work of Wren.

at 175-6 NEW BOND STREET, LONDON: *Cartier* Ltd

I

See map on page IV

Jaeger House, 204-206 Regent Street, London, W.1

Alpaca

Bactrian camel

Angora goat

Cashmere goat

Vicuna

Merino sheep

The House of Jaeger lead the world in wool fashions.   They never compromise on quality.
They use only the purest wool made from the finest animal fibres.   Their designers — the
best in Britain — give to all they do that stamp of distinction which is Jaeger's own.   So that
Jaeger has come to be, both within the trade and to the public, " the fashion name for wool."

JAEGER *The Fashion Name for Wool*

See map on page IV   II

The Landmark
of Fashionable London

Today, as 160 years ago, women of good taste come to Debenham & Freebody in Wigmore Street for the latest styles,

the finest silks, fabrics, muslins and lace — indeed, for all their fashion needs.   Generation after Generation, Daughter

has followed Mother to this most elegant of fashion houses, finding not merely impeccable quality, craftsmanship and

styles but traditionally British courtesy and comfort.   Every woman who comes to London should put a visit to

Debenham & Freebody early in her programme.

Bond Street is the nearest Underground Station.
Bus Routes 59 and 159.

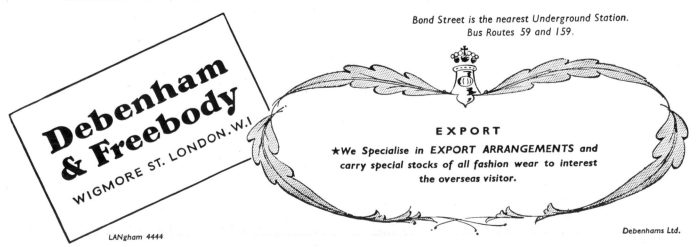

Debenham & Freebody
WIGMORE ST. LONDON. W.1

LANgham 4444

EXPORT
★We Specialise in EXPORT ARRANGEMENTS and
carry special stocks of all fashion wear to interest
the overseas visitor.

Debenhams Ltd.

See map on page IV

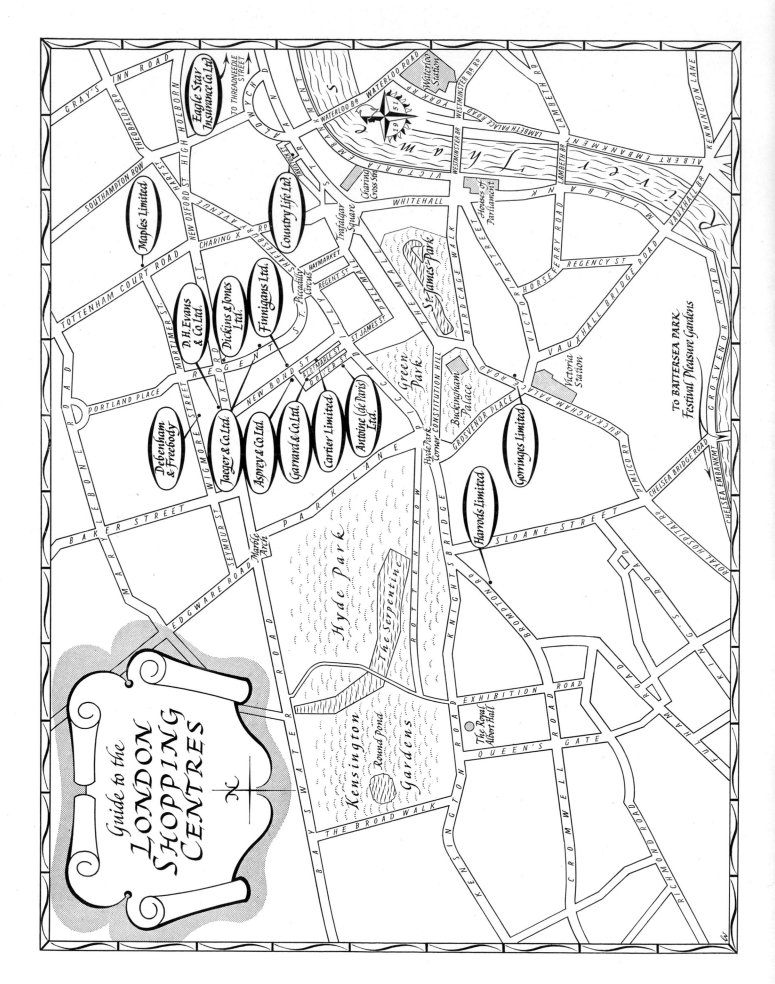

Guide to the
LONDON
SHOPPING
CENTRES

For many generations discriminating women have shopped at DICKINS and JONES. Since 1803 this name has symbolized distinguished, beautiful clothes and a pleasant courteous atmosphere in which to buy them. Today DICKINS and JONES, though very much aware of current trends, still maintains, as it did then, a position of unrivalled leadership in the world of London fashion

In 1835

BY APPOINTMENT

SILK MERCERS

In 1903

DICKINS AND JONES

REGENT STREET LONDON W.1

V

See map on page IV

Eagle Star Insurance Company Ltd,

1 Threadneedle Street, London, E.C.2.

THE OFFICES OF COUNTRY LIFE. Erected in 1904, this was the first public building to be designed by the late Sir Edwin Lutyens, and clearly shows the influence of Wren. It houses the combined editorial staffs of COUNTRY LIFE and its associated publications.

London's most modern shop - not only in structure but in
outlook - D.H.Evans caters for the woman of taste in every
income group. Our special pride is the size and variety
of our stocks of merchandise : beautiful, wearable clothes
are to be found at every price and in fittings and colours
to suit every type.   Our assistants are helpful and
resourceful : the Restaurant and Hairdressing Department are
there to make your day easy and effortless. The whole of
D.H.Evans is designed to make shopping a pleasure.

D. H. EVANS

OXFORD STREET W.1.

See map on page IV